Foundations of Sentient Marketing

What is Sentient Marketing? 6
AI in Modern Marketing 7
The Rise of Sentient Marketing 8
Why is Sentient Marketing Important? 8
Core Components of Sentient Marketing 9
Conclusion 10
Understanding the Foundations 12
Why is Sentiment Marketing so powerful? 12
Data-driven Decision Making 13
Analyzing for Insights 13
Real-Time Adaptation and Learning 14
Responsive Strategies 14
Dealing with the Luddites' Legacy 14
Building Trust and Transparency in Sentient Marketing 16
Ethical Considerations 17
Empathy and Connection 17
Personalization and Customer Experience 18
Customized Engagement 18
Enhancing Customer Journey 18
Chapter 3: Ethical Practices in Sentient Marketing 19
Transparency and Clarity 19
Cultivating Trust through Openness 19
Navigating Privacy and Compliance 20
Advancing Personalization and Consumer Empowerment 20
Conclusion: A Steadfast Ethical Commitment 20
Key Components 22
Trigger-based Marketing 22
Applying Triggers Across the Campaign Lifecycle 23
Conclusion 24
Case Study 1: Target - Predictive Analytics in Retail 27
Background 27

Implementation	27
Data Collection	27
Predictive Modeling	27
Personalized Marketing	27
Results & Consequences	27
Increased Sales	27
Customer Engagement	27
Breach of Trust	27
Case Study Assessment	27
Case Study 2: StitchFix - Customization and Personalization at Scale	27
Background	28
Style Profiling	28
Machine Learning	28
High Customization	28
Customer Retention	29
Operational Efficiency	29
Case Study Assessment	29
Case Study 3: YW Istanbul - Innovative Social Media Strategies	29
Background	29
Implementation Details	30
Sentiment Analysis	30
Targeted Campaigns	30
Dynamic Interaction	30
Results	30
Increased Bookings	30
Improved Reputation Management	31
Ethical Considerations and Best Practices	31
Case Study Assessment	31
Transparency	32
Clear Disclosure	32
Consent Record	33
Explicit Agreement and Respecting Customer Privacy	34
Values-Driven Marketing	35

    Societal Benefit — 35

Authenticity — 36

Long-term Engagement — 36

Integrating Ethics with Innovation — 36

Conclusion — 37

Foster a Data-Driven Culture — 38

    Collect Comprehensive Data — 38

Learn to Leverage Advanced Analytics — 40

    Implement Predictive Analytics — 40

Start Personalizing Customer Experiences — 41

    Dynamic Personalization — 41

Step 4: Integrate AI and Automation — 42

    Chatbots and Virtual Assistants — 42

Social Media Automation — 44

Step 5: Monitor and Optimize — 44

    Performance Metrics — 44

Common Pitfalls and How to Avoid Them — 46

    Over-Reliance on Technology — 46

    Collaboration with IT — 46

Conclusion — 47

Defining a Sentient Enterprise — 48

    Sensing Capabilities — 48

    Processing Information — 48

    Responding to Insights — 48

Implementing Sentient Technologies — 49

    Assessment and Planning — 49

    Building Capabilities — 49

    Integration and Deployment — 49

    Continuous Monitoring and Improvement — 50

The Benefits of Becoming a Sentient Enterprise — 50

    Enhanced Efficiency — 51

    Improved Customer Experiences — 51

    Competitive Advantage — 51

Conclusion	51
Fostering a Culture of Innovation	53
Building a Data-Driven Organization	54
Structuring for Agility	54
Continuous Learning and Development	54
Support During Transition	55
Conclusion	55
Predictive Technologies and AI	56
Advanced Predictive Analytics	56
AI-Powered Customer Insights	57
The Role of Automation in Marketing	57
AI-Driven Chatbots and Virtual Assistants	57
Hyper-Personalization	58
Granular Customer Segmentation	58
Dynamic Content Creation	59
Ethical AI and Responsible Marketing	59
Ethical AI Development	59
Consumer Privacy and Data Protection	60
The Impact of Emerging Technologies	60
Internet of Things (IoT)	60
Blockchain Technology	61
Preparing for the Future	61
Investing in Technology	61
Adapting to Change	62
Conclusion	62
Embrace Technology Without Losing Humanity	63
The Power of Human Connection	63
The Ethical Stewardship of Technology	64
Celebrating Human Ingenuity	64
Conclusion	65

Chapter 1: Introduction to Sentient Marketing

In the context of Artificial Intelligence, the term "sentient" is often misunderstood or misapplied. It suggests a level of consciousness or self-awareness that AI systems do not possess. AI can analyze data and make decisions based on programming and algorithms, but it lacks the capacity for emotions, subjective experiences, or self-awareness that characterizes sentient beings. Describing AI as "sentient" can lead to confusion and unrealistic expectations about its capabilities and future development.

In the context of marketing, "sentient" refers to an intelligence that is not just reactive but also innately self-aware and adaptive to changing circumstances. AI technologies possess the remarkable capability to act autonomously and evolve with new conditions. When integrated into marketing strategies, AI can profoundly transform processes and enhance the customer experience in ways we are only beginning to understand.

What is Sentient Marketing?

As we venture into this transformative era, Sentient Marketing promises to revolutionize not just how brands communicate, but also how they connect on an emotional level with each consumer. This approach considers the nuances of individual preferences, past interactions, and future needs, creating a seamless and intuitive consumer experience.

The power of Sentient Marketing lies in its ability to adapt in real-time. It uses continuous feedback loops from consumer actions to refine and personalize marketing messages further. This ongoing adaptation ensures that each consumer feels uniquely recognized and valued, fostering a deep sense of loyalty and engagement.

Moreover, Sentient Marketing empowers brands to anticipate needs before they are explicitly expressed. By analyzing behavioral data and emerging patterns, brands can proactively offer solutions, enhancing customer satisfaction and preemptively solving problems. This proactive approach not only streamlines the customer journey but also positions brands as thoughtful leaders in their industry.

Ultimately, Sentient Marketing transcends traditional marketing boundaries. It creates a dynamic dialogue between consumers and brands, where each interaction enriches the understanding and strengthens the bond. This strategy not only maximizes marketing efficiency but also elevates the entire customer experience, making every engagement an opportunity to delight and inspire.

As we embrace this promising future, the possibilities are limitless. Sentient Marketing is not just a tool but a gateway to a more connected and personalized world, where every marketing initiative is an insightful, heartfelt conversation with your audience.

AI in Modern Marketing

Modern marketing relies on large data sets to strategically target their market. The ability to respond swiftly to customer behaviors and trends in real time allows for continuous optimization, eliminating guesswork. Marketing teams can understand why something worked without additional questions and speculation, enabling better allocation of resources. This process helps businesses stay competitive, improve their services, and ultimately achieve better outcomes.

Sentient Marketing goes above and beyond current AI trends in contemporary marketing, as it strives to be more self-aware and self-correcting. While that sounds like the goal of Sentient Marketing is to remove humans, nothing could be further from the truth.

Intrigued? Keep on reading.

The Rise of Sentient Marketing

Sentient Marketing allows businesses to anticipate trends and deliver personalized experiences that resonate with their audience Utilizing real-time data and adaptive strategies.

As consumer expectations evolve, delivering personalized and timely interactions becomes crucial for building lasting relationships and driving brand loyalty. Sentient Marketing drives this evolution by merging cutting-edge technology with profound insights into human behavior, fostering a truly customer-centric approach.

Why is Sentient Marketing Important?

Sentient Marketing is a transformative approach that reshapes how businesses understand and connect with their consumers. By harnessing the power of AI, this method decodes consumer behaviors with unprecedented accuracy. Marketers can now target their efforts with precision, ensuring that their messages resonate deeply with the audience. This precision is like having a map that not only shows where customers are but also predicts where they're headed.

Moreover, Sentient Marketing enhances how businesses engage with their audiences. It transforms interactions by understanding and responding to consumer emotions and behaviors as if someone could read your diary and anticipate your needs with genuine empathy. This personal touch not only creates a deep sense of understanding but also fosters loyalty, transforming casual buyers into devoted fans who eagerly support the brand.

Additionally, AI-driven insights streamline marketing strategies, making them more efficient than ever before. This optimization eliminates wasted efforts on unresponsive audiences and ensures that every marketing move is strategically targeted. As a result, businesses maximize their return on investment and make their marketing expenditures more effective.

Overall, Sentient Marketing leverages the latest in AI technology to forge meaningful and impactful connections, allowing businesses to engage with their customers on a much deeper level. This method doesn't just reach an audience—it connects with them meaningfully, making every interaction valuable and memorable, and paving the way for a future where marketing feels like a conversation between old friends.

Sentient Marketing stands out as a transformative approach for several compelling reasons. By harnessing the power of advanced AI, businesses can now understand and anticipate customer needs with unparalleled accuracy. This innovative method moves beyond traditional marketing tactics, offering a more personalized and engaging experience that resonates on an emotional level. It's not just about delivering a message; it's about creating a dialogue that feels both natural and tailored to the individual.

Core Components of Sentient Marketing

To achieve these ends, marketers must understand the four core components of Sentient Marketing.

Data-Driven Decision Making: It's about using the mountain of consumer data at your fingertips to make intelligent, informed marketing decisions. This isn't guesswork—it's precision-crafted from insights gleaned from data.

Real-Time Adaptation and Learning: Picture your marketing strategies dynamically evolving in real-time, swiftly adapting to every consumer interaction. It's like having a campaign that's always on its toes, keeping you responsive and in tune with your audience.

Integration of AI and Machine Learning: We're talking about using cutting-edge algorithms to predict consumer behavior and automate responses. It's not just smart; it's predictive and proactive, helping you stay ahead of the curve.

Emotion Prompts: Understanding what makes your audience tick emotionally can transform engagement and boost conversion rates. It's about striking the right chord at the right moment, creating a deeper connection and fostering loyalty.

These components together create a marketing strategy that's not just smart but deeply intuitive, allowing you to connect with your audience in a meaningful and impactful way.

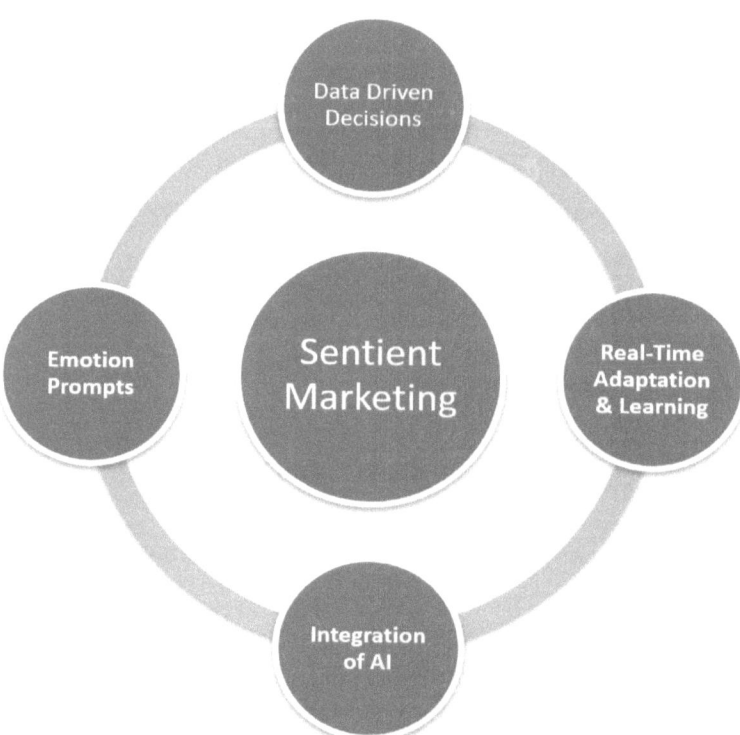

Figure 1: Sentient Marketing Components

Conclusion

Sentient Marketing is the most human-centric campaign strategy out there. AI isn't meant to replace humans but to augment what we can do, enhancing our ability to create deeply personalized and meaningful customer experiences at scale.

By leveraging advanced analytics and machine learning, Sentient Marketing enables businesses to understand their customers on a profound level, anticipating their needs and preferences with remarkable accuracy. This approach not only fosters stronger customer relationships but also drives engagement and loyalty, as each interaction feels uniquely tailored and relevant. In a world where consumers crave authenticity and connection, Sentient Marketing stands out as a powerful tool for brands to truly resonate with their audience.

Chapter 2: Core Principles of Sentient Marketing

Understanding the Foundations

Sentient Marketing flips the traditional product marketing script on its head. Instead of creating a product and finding a market, this approach lets the market decide what it wants. It's about responding to customers' needs even before the product is developed—groundbreaking stuff. By leveraging data insights into customer shopping preferences and behaviors, businesses can precisely anticipate and meet these needs.

When a business adopts the Sentient Marketing approach, the entire business transforms dramatically. Enhancing the interactions between the customer and the company leads to significant improvements. This shift opens up new avenues for personalized marketing strategies, revolutionizing how businesses engage with their audiences and driving superior outcomes.

Why is Sentiment Marketing so powerful?

Sentient Marketing transcends traditional marketing methods by harnessing the power of artificial intelligence to create a dynamic, interactive, and highly personalized consumer experience. Unlike static campaigns, Sentient Marketing evolves with the consumer, responding to their preferences and behaviors in real-time. This adaptability ensures that every interaction is relevant and engaging, enhancing the overall customer journey.

Moreover, Sentient Marketing places the customer at the heart of its strategy, fostering a deeper connection between brands and their audiences. It moves beyond mere transactional exchanges to build meaningful relationships, recognizing that today's consumers seek authenticity and value in their engagements. By leveraging AI to understand and anticipate customer needs, Sentient Marketing empowers businesses to deliver experiences that resonate on a personal level, driving loyalty and long-term satisfaction.

At a time when we are all constantly bombarded with generic marketing messages, Sentient Marketing stands out by offering a bespoke approach. It transforms the way businesses communicate with their customers, making every touchpoint an opportunity to strengthen brand loyalty and enhance customer satisfaction. This human-centric approach not only sets brands apart but also paves the way for a new standard in marketing excellence.

Data-driven Decision Making

Reaching the pinnacle of precision marketing hinges on data. Businesses amass information from a variety of sources—your online clicks, the items you add to your cart, third-party data brokers, and the tracking cookies that follow your online journey. Sentient Marketing kicks off by gathering and analyzing these data points. This data, when compiled, provides a detailed understanding of consumer interests and behaviors, which is crucial for effective marketing strategies.

Armed with this comprehensive consumer profile, businesses can embark on a journey of crafting highly personalized marketing strategies. They can tailor their messages and products, leading to a transformation in their campaigns, making them more impactful and captivating. This is the power of data-driven marketing, inspiring businesses to reach new heights. This data-driven approach ensures that marketing efforts resonate deeply with the audience, fostering stronger connections and driving better results.

Analyzing for Insights

Sophisticated algorithms now take the helm, acting as digital wizards that sift through massive mountains of data to uncover patterns and trends. These once-hidden insights reveal the secrets of customers' digital behaviors. With this valuable information, businesses can now make data-driven decisions that are smart and informed, transforming their marketing strategies.

Real-Time Adaptation and Learning

Sentient Marketing's power lies in its ability to learn and adapt in real time. Unlike traditional campaigns that require time to adjust, Sentient Marketing evolves instantly based on the latest data, keeping messaging and offers relevant and compelling.

This adaptability is crucial for responding to seasonal trends, market demands, and shifts in consumer sentiment. For instance, during a major event, Sentient Marketing can quickly align strategies to engage audiences with timely content, enhancing the brand's relevance.

By continually analyzing interactions, Sentient Marketing becomes smarter, predicting future behaviors accurately. This proactive approach keeps businesses ahead, offering innovative solutions and anticipating customer needs before they arise. This ability to learn and adapt in real time is why we refer to it as "sentient."

Responsive Strategies

One of the core tenets, and quite frankly, the most incredible aspect of Sentient Marketing, is its real-time adaptability. As you interact with a brand, the system learns from your behavior and adjusts its strategies accordingly. Imagine you're browsing a website and showing interest in a particular product. A Sentient Marketing system notices this and immediately presents you with related products or special offers, creating a seamless and personalized shopping experience.

Dealing with the Luddites' Legacy

The term "Luddite" is often used to describe anyone who resists new technology. However, its origins trace back to a significant labor movement in the early 19th century, which arose in response to the threat mechanized manufacturing posed to the skilled craftsmen of that era.

The original Luddites were British weavers and textile workers who fiercely opposed the adoption of mechanized looms and knitting frames. These individuals were highly skilled artisans, having spent years honing their craft. Their livelihood was at risk because unskilled laborers could operate these machines, which diminished the value of their expertise. The economic strain of the Napoleonic Wars exacerbated their plight, making the competition from early textile factories particularly devastating.

In response, some weavers took drastic action. They began to break into factories, smashing the very machines that endangered their profession. They adopted the name "Luddites" in honor of Ned Ludd, a young apprentice who, according to legend, had destroyed a textile machine in 1779. This act of rebellion became a symbol of their resistance against industrialization's encroachment on their skilled trade.

Fast forward to today, and we see a parallel in the world of marketing with the rise of artificial intelligence. Just as the Luddites feared mechanization, many marketing professionals are wary of AI. The advent of AI-driven tools threatens to automate tasks that once required a human touch—content creation, data analysis, customer interaction, and even strategic decision-making.

Like the weavers of old, today's marketers have invested years mastering their craft. They pride themselves on their creativity, intuition, and understanding of human behavior. The rapid advancement of AI can seem like it's undermining these hard-earned skills. The fear is not just about job loss, but also about the devaluation of their expertise.

However, history also teaches us that resistance alone is not the solution. Instead of viewing AI as a threat, marketers can see it as an ally. AI can handle repetitive tasks and data crunching, freeing up marketers to focus on strategic and creative endeavors that truly require a human touch. Embracing AI can lead to more personalized and effective marketing strategies, leveraging the strengths of both humans and machines.

In the end, the lesson from the Luddites is clear: while new technology can be disruptive, it also offers opportunities for those willing to adapt and integrate these innovations into their skill set. For marketers, embracing AI could mean not just surviving but thriving in the next wave of technological advancement.

Building Trust and Transparency in Sentient Marketing

As we dive deeper into data-driven marketing tactics, it's crucial to understand the evolving relationship between humans and machines—a relationship that need not be antagonistic. Humans remain in control, only using machines to streamline tasks, which reflects the essence of sentient marketing. This field flourishes with human oversight, encouraging us to overcome past hesitations and harness the combined strengths of human intelligence and automation's ability to handle routine tasks. We will see that illustrated beautifully in one of the case studies.

At the heart of Sentient Marketing lies the fusion of technology and the human element. Neither can succeed without the other. Sentient Marketing thrives on customer trust. Without customers' willingness to share data on their buying and browsing behaviors, there would be no data to analyze. Yet, the more they share, the more intelligent our systems become, making the marketing increasingly relevant.

Transparency in how businesses collect and use this data is critical, as it fosters trust with customers and paves the fastest route to brand loyalty. When customers feel secure in their online interactions with a brand, that brand's strategies become significantly more effective.

As technology advances sentient marketing, maintaining clarity about data usage and building trust with consumers is essential. Businesses must be transparent about their data practices and ensure consumers feel safe during their interactions.

Trust is the cornerstone; without it, even the most innovative and meticulously tested strategies might fail to connect.

Cultivating trust with consumers is fundamental to forging genuine relationships, boosting brand loyalty, and securing long-term success. In an era where distrust often comes first, customers are skeptical and highly selective. Earning and preserving their trust will set a brand apart, not just for growth but for scalability and sustainability.

Ethical Considerations

With great power comes great responsibility—the timeless mantra applies ever so poignantly to the world of data collection and usage. Upholding your privacy and sticking rigorously to data protection laws isn't just about fulfilling legal requirements; it's a profound moral commitment. Sentient Marketing navigates the delicate balance between cutting-edge innovation and ethical integrity by managing your information with the utmost care and respect. This approach isn't just the right thing to do; it's essential for building lasting, trust-based relationships with consumers.

Empathy and Connection

Fundamentally, marketing is about relationships—their needs, desires, and pain points. Sentient Marketing uses data to gain deep insights, but empathy turns these insights into meaningful actions. By genuinely connecting with consumers, businesses can create experiences that resonate on a personal level. This human touch transforms marketing from a transactional activity into a relationship-building endeavor.

Personalization and Customer Experience

Customized Engagement

Delivering highly individualized experiences involves more than just targeted ads; it also includes customized emails with bespoke product recommendations and made-to-order shopping experiences. Sentient Marketing creates detailed profiles for each individual, allowing for engagements that are uniquely adapted to their preferences. This strategy enhances the relevance of marketing efforts, making consumers feel truly understood and valued. As a result, customers are more likely to engage with the brand, leading to higher conversion rates and stronger customer loyalty.

Enhancing Customer Journey

From the first moment you interact with a brand to long after your purchase, Sentient Marketing enhances every step of your journey. By continuously learning from your interactions, businesses can ensure that each touchpoint is optimized for engagement and satisfaction. For example, if a customer shows interest in a particular product, Sentient Marketing can send follow-up emails with related products, special offers, or helpful content. Post-purchase, it can provide personalized recommendations for accessories or complementary products, keeping the customer engaged and encouraging repeat business.

This seamless integration of personalization throughout the customer journey transforms the shopping experience. Whether it's through timely and relevant content, proactive customer service, or tailored promotions, Sentient Marketing makes every interaction meaningful. This approach not only meets but exceeds customer expectations, turning one-time buyers into loyal advocates. By leveraging the power of AI to understand and anticipate customer needs, businesses can deliver a customer experience that feels truly bespoke, fostering a deeper connection and building long-term relationships.

Chapter 3: Ethical Practices in Sentient Marketing

Adopting ethical practices is not only required in the field of sentient marketing, but it also gives businesses a competitive edge that builds enduring relationships with customers. A dynamic approach that strikes a balance between precision in personalization and an unwavering commitment to privacy is necessary, given the constantly changing landscape of consumer data use and personalization.

Transparency and Clarity

Transparency is the fundamental tenet of ethical sentient marketing. Transparent and easily accessible communication about data use is essential to every interaction. Businesses should eschew technical legalese in favor of clear explanations that describe the different kinds of data that are gathered, how they are used, and the immediate advantages that they provide to customers. By using visual tools like infographics and FAQs, businesses can help consumers become more knowledgeable, gain a deeper sense of trust, and demystify data practices.

Cultivating Trust through Openness

Any effective marketing plan must be built on trust, especially in the digital age when data is king. Frequent transparency reports inform customers about data practices and AI applications while acting as open declarations of a business's continued dedication to moral business conduct. Initiatives for educating consumers, such as webinars and workshops, strengthen trust by improving knowledge and comfort with these practices. By showing that a company values its customers' privacy and security above all else, proactive approaches to problems like data breaches demonstrate a company's commitment to ethical practices and strengthen consumer trust.

Navigating Privacy and Compliance

In addition to being required by law, adherence to strict privacy standards and regulations, like the CCPA and GDPR, is essential to ethical marketing. Fairness is ensured and discrimination is prevented through proactive mitigation of biases in AI algorithms and routine audits, which demonstrate a company's commitment to moral business practices. A company's commitment to legal and ethical standards can be determined by how well it keeps up with regulatory changes and incorporates them into its daily operations.

Advancing Personalization and Consumer Empowerment

The use of AI innovations to deliver content that respects individual privacy and preferences, increases satisfaction, and builds loyalty, should be guided by ethics in the pursuit of personalization. Giving customers precise control over their personalization choices and data settings empowers them and fosters a sense of trust. When consumers feel they can control their digital interactions, engagement and satisfaction naturally follow.

Conclusion: A Steadfast Ethical Commitment

Sustaining strong and reliable consumer relationships requires sentient marketers to uphold the highest ethical standards. This all-encompassing strategy calls for more than just regulatory compliance and efficient communication; it also calls for a dedication to cutting-edge personalization strategies and respect for the rights of consumers and their privacy. Businesses that follow these guidelines not only successfully negotiate the challenges of digital marketing, but also win the respect and confidence of their clientele, which guarantees long-term prosperity and sustainability in the online market.

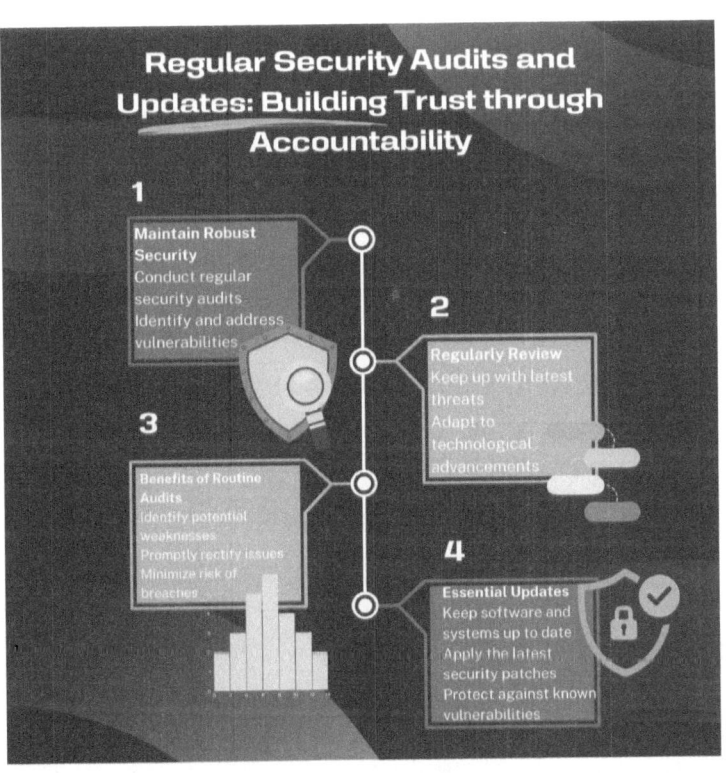

Chapter 4: Emotional Intelligence in AI Marketing

Imagine a world where your favorite brands understand what you crave and how you feel. Emotional intelligence in AI marketing makes this possible by using artificial intelligence to detect, analyze, and respond to human emotions in digital interactions. This capability allows businesses to connect more deeply with their audience, understanding and reacting to the emotional contexts of their communications and behaviors.

Key Components

Emotion recognition technologies, powered by AI, utilize both natural language processing (NLP) and machine learning to analyze the tone and sentiment of textual communications. This includes social media posts, customer reviews, and support tickets. Additionally, voice recognition systems assess the tones of calls to gauge emotions such as frustration, satisfaction, or confusion.

AI systems also perform behavioral analysis by examining user behaviors, including browsing patterns and purchase history, to infer emotional states and preferences. For instance, abrupt changes in buying behavior might indicate dissatisfaction or a change in personal circumstances.

Based on these insights, AI can adapt interactions by guiding the timing and tone of marketing messages. If a customer expresses dissatisfaction, the system might trigger support outreach with a compassionate tone or offer personalized discounts to mend the relationship.

Trigger-based Marketing

Trigger-based marketing leverages emotional triggers to motivate customers to make decisions, whether that is to buy, upgrade, or take some action. This approach taps into the psychological drivers that influence consumer behavior, ensuring that marketing efforts resonate on a deeper level. By understanding and utilizing these emotional triggers, businesses can effectively drive customers to their action threshold—the critical point at which they decide to take the desired action.

Applying Triggers Across the Campaign Lifecycle

By identifying emotional triggers through data analysis, marketers can craft impactful messages that significantly influence their campaign goals. Trigger-based marketing aims to increase engagement and conversion rates through messaging designed to evoke a response from the audience. Here's how it can be applied to different objectives:

Brand Awareness: The goal is to increase recognition and familiarity. Emotional triggers such as nostalgia, curiosity, or humor can make your brand memorable. For instance, a campaign evoking fond memories can connect deeply with audiences, enhancing brand recall and fostering a sense of loyalty.

Product Launch: Introducing a new product aims to generate excitement and interest. Triggers related to novelty and innovation are key. Highlighting cutting-edge technology or unique features can appeal to the audience's desire for the latest offerings, sparking initial engagement and curiosity.

Lead Generation: Capturing interest and gathering contact information is the objective. Urgency and exclusivity work well here. Offering a limited-time free trial or exclusive early access can prompt potential leads to act quickly to avoid missing out, thereby increasing the likelihood of conversion.

Sales Increase: Driving purchases and boosting sales figures benefit from triggers like scarcity and social proof. Ads highlighting limited stock or showcasing testimonials create urgency and trust, encouraging immediate purchases and enhancing customer satisfaction.

Integrating these emotional triggers into your marketing strategy can create compelling messages tailored to your campaign goals, driving better engagement and conversion rates. Additionally, the power of automation enables efficient implementation of these strategies. Marketing systems can automatically send messages based on specific behaviors or milestones. For example, an e-commerce store can celebrate a customer's loyalty program achievement with a congratulatory message and a special discount code, enhancing engagement and strengthening their connection to the brand.

Ethical Considerations: With the heavy reliance on consumer data and AI, ethical considerations are paramount. Businesses must prioritize consumer privacy, data protection, and transparency to foster trust and uphold a positive brand image. Responsible data handling and transparency are the cornerstones of ethical marketing practices, providing reassurance and confidence to all stakeholders.

Conclusion

Embracing the principles of sentient marketing, augmented by emotional intelligence, will transform business-customer interactions. Businesses that adopt these principles enhance customer satisfaction and loyalty, securing a competitive edge. By integrating emotions into marketing strategies, businesses forge deeper connections with customers, driving growth in a personalized and ethical way.

Prioritizing transparency, minimizing data collection, ensuring security, moderating personalization, rectifying AI biases, and upholding accountability are crucial for sustaining consumer confidence and building a future of marketing based on trust and respect. This approach not only boosts engagement and conversion rates but also establishes a sustainable and ethical marketing practice that benefits both businesses and consumers.

Chapter 5: Sentient Marketing Case Studies

There are more real world examples every day of successful sentient, marketing practices, and principles that Businesses are experimenting with. Let's dive into a couple real world examples, highlighting how data driven and AI inspired strategies can revolutionize business outcomes.

Case Study 1: Target - Predictive Analytics in Retail

Background

Target, one of the largest retail chains in the United States, aimed to revolutionize its customer shopping experience and boost sales through predictive analytics. Recognizing the potential of data-driven insights, Target sought to understand and anticipate customer needs, particularly around key life events that significantly influence purchasing behavior.

Implementation

With a solid data centric approach to mine for insights, Target put themselves on a path to success and controversy.

Data Collection

Target launched a comprehensive data collection initiative, gathering vast amounts of information from customer purchases, online browsing behaviors, and loyalty programs. By analyzing this data, Target gained a deeper understanding of individual customer preferences and shopping patterns.

Predictive Modeling

Target developed sophisticated predictive models using machine learning algorithms. These models identified and predicted purchasing behaviors, focusing on significant life events, such as pregnancy. By analyzing patterns in purchasing data, Target pinpointed subtle changes that often precede major life events, allowing them to anticipate customer needs before they were explicitly stated.

Personalized Marketing

Armed with insights from their predictive models, Target implemented a personalized marketing strategy. They sent tailored coupons and special offers to customers identified as being in the early stages of pregnancy. These personalized communications included discounts on baby products and related items, meeting the specific needs of expectant parents. This approach enhanced the shopping experience and strengthened customer loyalty by demonstrating a keen understanding of their unique needs.

Results & Consequences

On the surface, this campaign was a smashing success. However, this success came at a price.

Increased Sales

Using predictive analytics, Target significantly boosted sales of baby products. By accurately predicting and meeting the needs of expectant parents, Target captured a larger share of this important market segment.

Customer Engagement

Target's personalized marketing approach significantly enhanced customer engagement. Customers appreciated the relevant and timely offers, which made their shopping experience more convenient and enjoyable. This increased engagement drove immediate sales and fostered long-term loyalty, as customers felt understood and valued by the retailer.

Breach of Trust

However, the personalized marketing approach had unintended, even "creepy," consequences. The issue of pregnancy is quite sensitive, and when Target was trying to do something nice, it backfired. Customers began to distrust Target with their data after a high-profile incident where an expectant teenager's pregnancy was revealed to her family through Target's marketing.

This breach of trust took Target years to recover from, highlighting the risks associated with predictive analytics when not handled with sensitivity and transparency. And, to this day, it remains a cautionary tale in customer analytics and privacy conversation.

Case Study Assessment

By leveraging predictive analytics, Target successfully transformed its marketing strategy, leading to improved sales and deeper customer relationships. However, the case also illustrates the critical importance of handling customer data with care and maintaining trust. Additionally, it raises the importance of subtlety in applying what has been learned through analyzing data to avoid appearing invasive or even unnerving.

Ethical considerations and transparency are paramount in predictive analytics to avoid breaches of trust and ensure long-term customer loyalty.

Case Study 2: StitchFix - Customization and Personalization at Scale

In this case study, discover how humans play an essential role of Sentient Marketing.

Background

Stitch Fix, an online styling service, uses AI to personalize clothing selections based on customer preferences and feedback. By combining advanced algorithms with human expertise, Stitch Fix aims to deliver a highly customized shopping experience that meets each customer's unique tastes and needs.
Implementation

Style Profiling

Stitch Fix starts by having customers fill out detailed style profiles, capturing preferences for clothing styles, sizes, and other personal fashion preferences. This information feeds into their AI algorithm, forming the foundation for personalized clothing recommendations.

Machine Learning

The invaluable customer feedback is at the heart of Stitch Fix's machine learning algorithms. After each purchase and interaction, this feedback is analyzed, refining future selections and ensuring the AI evolves with each interaction. The algorithms adeptly detect patterns and trends in buying behaviors, size, style, and aesthetics.

High Customization

Each customer is treated to a unique blend of AI and human stylist expertise. The AI generates initial recommendations, which are then meticulously reviewed and adjusted by human stylists. This collaborative approach ensures the selections align perfectly with the customer's preferences, offering a level of customization that is both personal and precise, a hallmark of Stitch Fix's service.
Results:

Customer Retention

Stitch Fix has achieved high retention rates due to its tailored shopping experience. Customers appreciate the personalized attention and the convenience of receiving clothing items that match their unique style preferences, leading to higher satisfaction and loyalty.

Operational Efficiency

By leveraging AI, Stitch Fix has improved inventory management and reduced returns. Accurately predictions and personalized selections ensure customers are more likely to keep the items they receive, reducing the need for returns and exchanges. This efficiency enhances the customer experience and optimizes operational costs.

Case Study Assessment

Stitch Fix's successful implementation of AI-driven personalization demonstrates the power of combining technology with human insight to create a highly customized and efficient shopping experience. This case study highlights how businesses can leverage AI to scale personalization and enhance customer satisfaction and operational performance.

Case Study 3: YW Istanbul - Innovative Social Media Strategies

Background

YW Istanbul, a boutique hotel, utilized AI to enhance its social media marketing strategies. By leveraging advanced AI tools, YW Istanbul aimed to better understand and engage with potential customers, drive more direct bookings, and improve overall customer satisfaction.

Implementation Details

YW Istanbul took the phrase "Know Your Customer" to the next level by analyzing the needs, motivations, and tastes of their target customers.

Sentiment Analysis

YW Istanbul employed AI tools to analyze online reviews and social media mentions, gauging customer sentiment. This analysis provided valuable insights into guest preferences and areas needing improvement, allowing the hotel to tailor its marketing strategies effectively.

Targeted Campaigns

Using insights from sentiment analysis, YW Istanbul developed targeted ads and promotional content to attract new visitors. These campaigns were crafted to resonate with potential customers' preferences and emotions, enhancing the effectiveness of their marketing efforts.

Dynamic Interaction

AI-driven chatbots provide real-time assistance to potential customers on social media platforms. These chatbots improved engagement by answering questions, offering personalized recommendations, and assisting with bookings, creating a seamless customer experience.

Results

Increased Bookings

YW Istanbul experienced a notable rise in direct bookings through its social media channels. The targeted campaigns and dynamic interactions significantly contributed to converting social media users into hotel guests.

Improved Reputation Management

Swift responses and tailored services offered through AI-driven interactions enhanced overall customer satisfaction. YW Istanbul effectively managed its online reputation by addressing concerns and highlighting positive feedback.

Ethical Considerations and Best Practices

Each case study underscores the importance of ethical considerations when using consumer data and AI. Emphasizing transparency, data protection, and ethical AI use is crucial to maintaining customer trust.

Case Study Assessment

These case studies illustrate the practical benefits of sentient marketing. By leveraging AI and machine learning, businesses can gain a deep understanding of their customers, leading to more effective and personalized marketing efforts. These examples serve as a blueprint for other businesses aiming to harness the power of sentient marketing, showing that the future of marketing is not just about understanding what customers want but also how they feel.

Chapter 6: Ethical Practices in AI-Driven Campaigns

For any Sentient Marketing practice to be successful the result has to not only meet your needs but also respect your values and privacy. Ethical marketing practices are not just a necessity for maintaining trust and integrity, especially when deploying AI-driven strategies, but they also bring significant benefits to businesses.

Let's explore how businesses can integrate ethics more deeply into their marketing approaches and make them a cornerstone of their brand, reaping the rewards of consumer trust and loyalty.

Transparency

The power of transparency and trust is central to the principles of sentient marketing.To fulfill this commitment, it's vital to ensure that data is collected and analyzed just for the purposes intended. Businesses should not access additional data. Usage practices are transparent, ethical, and fully respectful of consumer privacy.

Here's how this can be accomplished.

Transparency should be the guiding principle. When consumers interact with services, it is crucial to clearly outline what data is being collected and why it is needed. Communicating these details in plain language, free from legal jargon, helps consumers easily understand what they are agreeing to.

Clear Disclosure

It is crucial to let customers know when AI is in play. Whether it's customer service bots, personalized ads, or content curation, transparency about AI's role is the key to building trust. Emphasizing transparency can make your audience feel more secure and confident in your marketing practices.

> *Example*: An AI-powered health and wellness app informs users about the data it collects and how AI uses it to make personalized recommendations. Users are explicitly asked to opt-in to data sharing and can adjust their preferences anytime. This transparency helps users feel more in control and trusting of the app.

The importance of freely given consent cannot be overstated. Consumers must always have the choice to provide or withhold their data without any negative repercussions. Avoiding pre-ticked boxes or default consent settings ensures that consumers actively opt-in to share their information. This approach guarantees that consent is both informed and voluntary.

Consent forms should be crafted to provide detailed information about the data collection process. These forms must specify the types of data being collected, the purposes for which this data will be used, and any third parties with whom the data may be shared. Additionally, they should outline the duration for which the data will be retained.

Accessibility needs to be a key consideration. Consent forms and privacy policies should be created in multiple languages and be made inclusive and accessible to all. Not only is this the right thing to do, many jurisdictions require it.

Consent Record

To uphold the commitment to transparency, it is essential to meticulously record all consents received. Storing these records securely and making them easily retrievable helps consumers review their consent history when needed. Implementing these principles involves a few crucial steps. It is important to collaborate closely with the legal and marketing teams to draft consent forms that meet all regulatory requirements while remaining user-friendly. UX/UI designers should work diligently to create interfaces that facilitate easy consent management.

Additionally, providing educational materials—such as videos, FAQs, and guides—can help consumers understand the importance of consent and how to manage their data preferences.

Finally, regularly monitoring consent collection processes and conducting audits ensures that best practices are implemented and updated as needed. This ongoing vigilance helps maintain the highest standards of privacy and trust.

By embedding these principles into every aspect of operations, marketers can build relationships of trust and respect with their communities, ensuring that consumer data is always handled with the utmost care. This approach not only honors the principles of Sentient Marketing but also fosters a more ethical and transparent digital environment.

Explicit Agreement and Respecting Customer Privacy

Ensuring explicit agreement from consumers for data collection and usage is paramount. Always obtain clear and informed consent from consumers, making sure the information provided is easy to understand. Consent should be given freely, without any pressure or ambiguity. This approach not only complies with legal requirements but also builds trust with your audience, showing them that their privacy is respected and valued.

Respecting customer privacy goes beyond mere compliance with laws such as GDPR. It involves making customer privacy a fundamental practice within your organization. Implement robust data protection measures to safeguard personal information and consistently respect user preferences regarding data sharing. By doing so, you demonstrate a commitment to ethical data handling and reinforce the trust customers place in your brand.

Incorporating these practices into your data strategy ensures that your organization not only meets regulatory standards but also upholds the highest ethical standards. This commitment to privacy and transparency strengthens customer relationships and enhances your brand's reputation.

Values-Driven Marketing

Sentient Marketing leverages the latest in AI technology to forge meaningful and impactful connections, allowing businesses to engage with their customers on a deeper level. This method doesn't just reach an audience—it connects with them meaningfully, making every interaction valuable and memorable, and paving the way for a future where marketing feels like a conversation between old friends. By harnessing advanced AI, businesses can now understand and anticipate customer needs with unparalleled accuracy. This innovative approach moves beyond traditional tactics, offering a more personalized and engaging experience that connects on an emotional level. It's not just about delivering a message; it's about creating a dialogue that feels both natural and tailored to the individual.

Societal Benefit

When you tie your marketing campaigns to societal benefits like promoting wellness, environmental sustainability, or social responsibility, you're not just enhancing your brand image; you're also contributing to broader societal goals. This inspiring approach can make you feel like you're making a real difference with your marketing strategies.

> *Example*: A sustainable clothing brand uses AI to analyze fashion trends and customer feedback to create stylish, eco-friendly clothing. The marketing highlights the brand's commitment to reducing waste and using ethically sourced materials, appealing to consumers who value sustainability. Real customer stories about how the clothing has positively impacted their lives reinforce the brand's authentic commitment to customer value.

Authenticity

Imagine marketing campaigns built on real customer testimonials, backed by solid scientific data, and driven by transparent business practices. There's no room for exaggerated claims or false expectations here. Instead, every message builds trust with honesty and integrity, creating a bond with each customer. This kind of authenticity not only attracts but also keeps people coming back, feeling confident and valued. It's about being real, being trustworthy, and letting your true colors shine through in every interaction.

Long-term Engagement

Focus on long-term customer relationships through consistent value delivery and regular engagement. This approach fosters loyalty and reinforces the benefits of staying connected with your brand. By consistently providing value and maintaining regular communication, you build strong, lasting relationships that benefit both your customers and your business.

Integrating Ethics with Innovation

By directly integrating ethical considerations into their AI strategies, businesses can prevent potential backlash and foster stronger, more loyal customer relationships. Ethical marketing should be seen not just as a compliance or CSR effort, but as a core part of a brand's value proposition. This approach empowers your brand to stand out in a crowded market and maintain control of your marketing narrative.

Conclusion

Incorporating these ethical principles into your marketing strategies ensures that you're not just reaching out to your customers but also respecting and valuing them and their privacy. It's about creating a future where marketing and ethics go hand in hand, building a trusted and respected brand.

By embedding these principles into the core of your brand's value proposition, you prevent potential backlash and build stronger customer relationships. This integration ensures that your marketing efforts are not only effective but also ethical, distinguishing your business in a crowded market and maintaining control over your marketing narrative.

Chapter 7: How to Implement a Sentient Marketing Practice

As stated before, implementing a Sentient Marketing practice requires a strategic approach integrating advanced technologies, marketing expertise, and an emphasis on ethical choices. Let's walk through the essential steps to make this a reality.

Foster a Data-Driven Culture

Businesses have always been collecting data, whether in a database, spreadsheet, or leather bound ledger. Data has always been here and, as such, we tend to take it for granted and ignore the wisdom hidden within. Over the last two decades or so, smart marketers and entrepreneurs have discovered the transformative power of mining data for patterns and opportunities. As such, many traditional business models have been disrupted and established market leaders have been sidelined by smaller, more nimble, and data centric competitors.

If you think that the age of disruption has ended or stalled, then think again: we have not seen anything yet. Fostering a data-driven culture has become a mandatory aspect of a successful business. Culture takes some time to change. In this context, then the best time to start moving towards a data-driven approach is now.

Collect Comprehensive Data

Integrating data from diverse sources, such as CRM systems, social media, website analytics, and IoT devices, forms the cornerstone of sentient marketing. This comprehensive approach to data collection lays the foundation for understanding and responding to customer needs in real time.

Equally crucial is the quality of the data collected. Ensuring that data collection is both precise and thorough is essential, as reliable insights are derived from high-quality data. This meticulous attention to detail ensures that marketing strategies are not only informed but also effective, enabling businesses to connect with their customers in more meaningful ways.

Encourage Data Literacy

Encouraging data literacy starts with changing the culture of your organization. Onboarding and training programs that educate employees on data analysis and interpretation are essential steps. When your team comprehensively understands data, they are better equipped to leverage it effectively.

Making data accessible to all relevant departments is also critical in fostering a culture of data-driven decision-making. Broad access to data enables every department to make more informed and effective choices, ultimately enhancing overall organizational performance. By ensuring that data is available and understandable, you empower employees to use data insights in their everyday decision-making processes.

Training Programs: Provide employees with comprehensive training on data analysis and interpretation. This training should cover the basics of data handling, how to interpret data trends, and how to apply these insights to their specific roles. When your team has a deep understanding of data, they can use it to drive better decisions and more innovative solutions. Investing in these programs ensures that all employees, regardless of their department, are proficient in data literacy.

Data Accessibility: Ensure that data is easily accessible to all relevant departments. Implementing user-friendly data platforms and dashboards can help in this regard. When data is accessible, departments can work more collaboratively and make decisions based on real-time information. This broad access breaks down silos within the organization, promoting a more integrated and cohesive approach to achieving business goals. By fostering an environment where data is readily available, you encourage a culture of transparency and accountability.

Overall, fostering data literacy within your organization transforms data from a mere tool into a strategic asset. This cultural shift enables employees at all levels to harness the power of data, driving innovation and performance across the board.

Learn to Leverage Advanced Analytics

Up until recently, advanced analytics were confined to academic, mathematical, or solely technical pursuits. Now, they are essential to building data-driven processes, companies, and cultures.

Implement Predictive Analytics

Utilizing advanced tools and technologies, such as predictive analytics, is crucial in modern marketing. By harnessing these insights, we can anticipate customer needs and tailor our marketing strategies accordingly. Such proactive practices are key to staying ahead of the curve, allowing businesses to adapt quickly and efficiently to changing consumer behaviors and market trends.

However, it's not just about gathering data—it's about transforming these insights into actionable marketing strategies. Understanding the data and knowing how to effectively utilize it is crucial for driving successful outcomes.

Machine learning is incredibly important in marketing. By creating custom algorithms designed for your business's specific needs, you ensure that artificial intelligence works effectively for your unique goals. Additionally, it's crucial that these algorithms keep learning and adapting based on new data. This ongoing improvement keeps your marketing strategies up-to-date and effective, constantly improving their impact over time.

Start Personalizing Customer Experiences

Segmentation plays a crucial role in refining marketing strategies. By creating detailed customer segments based on demographics, behaviors, and preferences, marketers can craft strategies that are specifically tailored to each group. This targeted approach ensures that marketing efforts are more effective, reaching and engaging each segment with precision.

Building on this foundation, targeted campaigns are then designed to cater to the unique characteristics of each segment. This allows for a more personalized marketing experience, increasing the relevance and impact of the campaigns.

Segmentation Customer Segments: Create detailed customer segments based on demographics, behaviors, and preferences. Tailored marketing strategies derived from this segmentation can reach and engage each group more effectively.

Targeted Campaigns: Design marketing campaigns tailored to each segment's unique characteristics.

Dynamic Personalization

Dynamic personalization is transforming how businesses engage with their customers. By implementing systems that adapt marketing messages in real-time based on customer interactions, businesses can ensure that the content they deliver is always relevant. This responsiveness to customer behavior enhances the effectiveness of marketing efforts.

Moreover, it's crucial to ensure that these personalized experiences are consistent across all touchpoints. Whether it's through email, social media, or in-app interactions, maintaining a unified approach across channels significantly enhances the overall customer experience. This multi-channel engagement strategy not only meets customers where they are but also builds a cohesive brand presence that resonates more deeply with them.

Dynamic Real-Time Personalization

Dynamic real-time personalization involves implementing systems that adapt marketing messages based on customer interactions. These systems continuously analyze customer behavior and preferences, allowing your marketing content to remain relevant and engaging. By responding to customer actions in real-time, you can deliver personalized experiences that resonate more deeply with your audience, fostering stronger connections and improving conversion rates.

Ensuring personalized experiences across all touchpoints is crucial for a cohesive customer journey. This means tailoring interactions not only through email but also across social media platforms, in-app experiences, and other digital channels. Consistency in personalization across these various touchpoints enhances the overall customer experience, making interactions with your brand feel seamless and intuitive.

By integrating real-time personalization with multi-channel engagement, you create a unified and engaging experience that meets customers where they are. This approach ensures that every interaction is meaningful and relevant, building loyalty and driving long-term customer satisfaction.

Step 4: Integrate AI and Automation

Chatbots and Virtual Assistants

Customer support and sales processes are becoming more efficient with the integration of AI technologies. Deploying AI-driven chatbots for customer support can handle inquiries around the clock, providing quick and accurate responses that enhance customer satisfaction. Similarly, virtual assistants can guide customers through the purchasing process, streamlining the sales journey and minimizing friction.

In the realm of marketing, automation plays a key role. Email automation allows businesses to send personalized content at optimal times, significantly improving engagement and increasing the likelihood of conversions. Furthermore, automating social media posts ensures that a business maintains consistent engagement with its audience. This not only keeps the social presence active and responsive but also frees up time for strategic planning and content creation.

Customer Support

Deploy AI-driven chatbots to handle customer inquiries and provide efficient support. These tools offer quick and accurate responses, addressing customer issues in real-time. By reducing wait times and improving the quality of interactions, chatbots significantly enhance customer satisfaction. Implementing these systems allows your support team to focus on more complex issues, ensuring a better overall service experience.

Sales Assistance

Utilize virtual assistants to guide customers through the purchasing process. These assistants can provide detailed product information, answer questions, and offer recommendations based on customer preferences. By streamlining the sales journey and reducing friction, virtual assistants help increase conversion rates. They ensure a smooth and personalized shopping experience, which boosts customer confidence and satisfaction.

Automated Marketing Email Automation

Automate email campaigns to deliver personalized content at optimal times. Using data-driven insights, these campaigns can be tailored to individual customer behaviors and preferences. Proper timing of these emails is crucial for maximizing engagement and conversions. Automation not only saves time but also enhances the effectiveness of your email marketing strategy by ensuring consistent and relevant communication.

Social Media Automation

Schedule and manage social media posts to maintain consistent engagement with your audience. Automation tools help you plan and execute your social media strategy efficiently. By ensuring that your social presence is always active and responsive, you can engage with your followers more effectively. This consistent engagement helps build a stronger online community and enhances your brand's visibility and reputation.

Step 5: Monitor and Optimize

Performance Metrics

Defining clear key performance indicators (KPIs) is crucial for measuring the success of Sentient Marketing initiatives. These metrics not only track progress but also highlight areas that may need improvement, guiding strategic decisions. Real-time monitoring is another essential component. Utilizing analytics dashboards allows teams to observe campaign performance as it unfolds, enabling quick adjustments and optimizations to enhance outcomes.

For continuous improvement, A/B testing is invaluable. By testing different marketing strategies against each other, businesses can identify the most effective tactics, continuously refining their approach. Additionally, establishing feedback loops to incorporate customer feedback into marketing strategies is vital. Listening to customers helps ensure that marketing efforts remain relevant and effectively meet their needs.

Key Performance Indicators (KPIs)

Define key performance indicators (KPIs) to measure the success of Sentient Marketing initiatives. Establishing clear metrics allows you to track progress accurately and identify areas needing improvement. These indicators provide a benchmark for evaluating the effectiveness of your strategies. Regularly reviewing KPIs ensures your marketing efforts align with your business objectives.

Real-Time Monitoring

Use analytics dashboards to monitor campaign performance in real-time. This capability allows you to make quick adjustments and optimizations based on live data. Real-time monitoring helps identify issues and opportunities promptly, ensuring your campaigns remain effective. By continuously observing performance, you can maintain the agility needed to adapt to changing market conditions.

Continuous Improvement

Conduct A/B tests to determine the most effective marketing strategies. By testing different approaches, you can refine and improve your tactics. This method helps identify what resonates best with your audience, leading to more successful campaigns. Continuous testing and iteration ensure your marketing stays relevant and effective.

Feedback Loops

Establish feedback loops to incorporate customer feedback into your marketing strategies. Listening to your customers provides valuable insights that keep your marketing relevant and practical. By actively seeking and integrating feedback, you can make informed adjustments that enhance customer satisfaction. This ongoing dialogue with customers fosters trust and loyalty, driving long-term success.

Common Pitfalls and How to Avoid Them

Over-Reliance on Technology

In AI-driven marketing, the harmonious balance between technology and human judgment becomes paramount. While AI offers valuable insights and data-driven strategies, humans' critical thinking and intuition truly guide these tools to their fullest potential. This synergy ensures that decisions are data-informed and deeply aligned with human values and societal norms.

The significance of ethical considerations cannot be overstated. As AI systems become more prevalent in marketing, ensuring their ethical use is crucial to prevent biases and misuse. By implementing ethical practices in AI-driven marketing, businesses foster trust and loyalty among consumers. When businesses commit to transparency and fairness, they create a foundation of reliability that resonates with their audience, making them feel reassured and confident.

One of the significant challenges in this domain is the lack of integration among various marketing systems and tools. Seamless integration is vital for enhancing operational efficiency and ensuring a smooth data flow. When all components of the marketing ecosystem are unified, they work together more effectively, driving better outcomes and more cohesive strategies.

Collaboration with IT

Equally vital is the spirit of collaboration among different teams within an organization. Fostering a collaborative environment between marketing, IT, and data science teams ensures that all aspects of intelligent marketing are well-coordinated. When these diverse teams come together, their combined expertise leads to innovative solutions and a more robust marketing approach. This teamwork not only streamlines processes but ultimately propels the organization towards greater success, inspiring and motivating the audience.

Conclusion

By implementing these strategies, businesses can develop marketing campaigns that better resonate with their customers. Regular monitoring and optimization are essential to staying ahead of evolving consumer behaviors and market trends, ensuring campaigns remain relevant and practical.

Chapter 8: The Sentient Enterprise

Imagine a business that reacts to and anticipates changes, adapting in real time like a living organism. A sentient enterprise transcends traditional AI use in marketing by integrating AI and machine learning across all functions to create a responsive, data-driven organization.

Defining a Sentient Enterprise

A sentient enterprise can sense, process, and respond to environmental changes in real time. It leverages AI, machine learning, and advanced analytics to make data-driven decisions, automate processes, and enhance efficiency.

Sensing Capabilities

Boost perceptive abilities by incorporating Internet of Things (IoT) devices to collect live data from various sources, including customer interactions, operational statistics, and market tendencies. Leverage sophisticated analytics to apply predictive models, forecasting future patterns and actions.

Processing Information

Data lakes act as vast digital repositories where businesses store enormous amounts of information, organized or not. These repositories make it easy to access and analyze data when needed. Machine learning models, continually learning and improving with new data, become increasingly intelligent and efficient, enabling businesses to make better decisions and predictions.

Responding to Insights

Responding to insights involves implementing AI systems capable of automated decision-making. It requires dynamically adjusting strategies and operations based on real-time data insights, ensuring businesses remain agile and responsive to changing conditions.

Implementing Sentient Technologies

With the definition of a Sentient Enterprise in place, how do businesses go about implementing the technology stack to make the transition. For starters, do not begin with haphazardly implementing new technology. Start with an assessment that will Inform your strategic planning.

Assessment and Planning

Start with a comprehensive technology audit to evaluate the organization's current technological landscape, identifying gaps and areas needing improvement. Develop a strategic roadmap detailing the plan for integrating new technologies, guiding the organization from its current state to a more advanced, technologically capable future.

Building Capabilities

Focus on talent acquisition and hiring data scientists, AI specialists, and other experts essential for developing and managing sentient technologies. Concurrently, invest in training programs to upskill existing employees, equipping them with knowledge and skills related to new technologies and data-driven practices. This dual approach builds a robust foundation for technological advancement.

Integration and Deployment

Start with small-scale projects to evaluate new technologies, collect crucial insights, and make needed modifications before a more comprehensive implementation. Slowly deploy the technologies throughout the organization to ensure a seamless transition and resolve any challenges that emerge during the rollout.

Continuous Monitoring and Improvement

Set up evaluation criteria to assess the impact of newly integrated sentient technologies, offering a numerical foundation for determining success and pinpointing areas needing enhancement. Develop feedback mechanisms to perpetually upgrade and adjust the technologies, routinely gathering performance metrics and user input to fine-tune and advance the technologies.

The Benefits of Becoming a Sentient Enterprise

Embracing the sentient enterprise model transforms a business's operational, customer, and competitive landscape. Leveraging advanced AI and data analytics, a sentient enterprise can streamline operations and increase efficiency, enabling precise decision-making, reducing costs, and improving productivity. Automation enhances efficiency, reducing manual effort and improving accuracy, allowing human resources to focus on strategic tasks. Real-time data insights enable faster decision-making, allowing organizations to respond promptly to opportunities and challenges.

On the customer front, adopting a conscious model enhances personalization and engagement. Advanced personalization delivers highly tailored services, enhancing satisfaction and engagement. Proactive customer service, driven by real-time data insights, addresses issues before they escalate, ensuring a seamless and supportive customer journey, building trust, and fostering long-term loyalty.

Competitively, a sentient enterprise gains an edge through continuous innovation and market responsiveness. By consistently refining business processes, organizations stay ahead of competitors, fostering a culture of growth and adaptation.

Enhanced Efficiency

Automation stands at the forefront of enhanced efficiency, significantly reducing manual effort and improving accuracy. By automating routine processes, organizations streamline operations, allowing human resources to focus on strategic tasks. Real-time data insights enable swift decision-making, ensuring prompt responses to opportunities and challenges.

Improved Customer Experiences

Becoming a conscious enterprise dramatically improves customer experiences. Advanced personalization allows businesses to deliver highly tailored services that meet individual customer needs, enhancing satisfaction and engagement. Proactive engagement enhances the customer experience by foreseeing potential problems and resolving them before they escalate, ensuring a smooth and supportive journey. This attentiveness builds trust and fosters long-term loyalty.

Competitive Advantage

A sentient enterprise excels through continuous innovation, consistently refining business processes to stay ahead of competitors. This constant evolution ensures the business remains at the cutting edge, capable of meeting the market's ever-changing demands. A sentient enterprise remains flexible, which is crucial; a sentient enterprise is agile and able to pivot in response to new trends and challenges, ensuring relevance and competitiveness.

Conclusion

Transforming into a sentient enterprise requires a strategic approach, significant technological investment, and a cultural shift toward data-driven decision-making. The advantages include increased efficiency, better customer interactions, and a lasting competitive edge. By adopting these technologies and principles, businesses can secure long-term success in a rapidly evolving environment. Sentient Marketing represents both a technological advancement and a fundamental shift in customer engagement.

Businesses can develop highly customized and efficient marketing strategies by employing AI, machine learning, and data analytics. This transformation demands continuous learning and adaptation, new technologies, and rethinking customer interaction approaches.

Sentient Marketing allows businesses to anticipate customer needs, tailor communications, and deliver services with unprecedented precision and relevance. Transitioning to a sentient enterprise involves committing to ethical practices and ensuring a strong focus on customer privacy, data security, and transparency.

Chapter 9: Aligning Organizational Culture and Structure for a Sentient Enterprise

To truly transform into a sentient enterprise, organizations must align their culture and structure with the principles of Sentient Marketing and AI-driven decision-making.

This chapter delves into strategies for cultivating an innovative environment, enhancing collaboration, and promoting continuous learning within your organization. It also provides insights into structuring your organization to effectively support these principles, ensuring a seamless integration of Sentient Marketing and enterprise-wide AI initiatives.

Fostering a Culture of Innovation

Cultivating a culture of innovation involves nurturing collaboration and ensuring robust leadership support, making innovation a core component of the organizational ethos. Encouraging experimentation is essential, as creating a safe-to-fail environment allows employees to try new ideas without fear of negative repercussions. Recognizing and rewarding innovative ideas through incentive programs motivates employees to think creatively.

Engaging leadership from all stakeholders fosters a culture that embraces innovation. Regular brainstorming sessions where employees from various departments exchange ideas lead to better solutions. Visible commitment from leadership, including providing necessary resources, is crucial for supporting and engaging in innovation initiatives.

Building a Data-Driven Organization

A data-driven organization relies on data literacy, accessibility, and decision-making frameworks to transform raw data into actionable insights. Comprehensive training programs improve data literacy across the organization, ensuring employees understand how to interpret and use data. Ensuring data accessibility promotes a unified approach to data use and breaks down silos, enabling effective data sharing.

Developing data-driven decision frameworks prioritizes decisions based on insights rather than intuition. Celebrating the impact of data-driven decisions by measuring and highlighting their success reinforces the value of this approach.

Structuring for Agility

Structuring an organization for agility involves flattening hierarchies and empowering teams to make swift, effective decisions. Reducing hierarchical layers promotes faster decision-making and more direct communication.

Empowering teams with the authority and autonomy to respond quickly to changing circumstances is essential. Adopting agile methodologies like Scrum or Kanban supports iterative development, flexibility, and continuous improvement,

Continuous Learning and Development

Encouraging lifelong learning and knowledge sharing fosters a collaborative environment. Offering comprehensive training programs covering both technical skills, such as AI and data analytics, and soft skills, such as collaboration and problem-solving, is essential.

Mentorship programs help employees learn from experienced colleagues, accelerating learning and professional growth. Effective change management involves transparent communication, feedback mechanisms, and support systems. Openly communicating about changes, including their reasons and expected benefits, builds trust and buy-in. Establishing mechanisms for employee feedback and using it to make adjustments improves the change management process.

Support During Transition

Training change champions within the organization helps drive change initiatives and support peers during transitions. Providing support systems such as counseling, coaching, and resources aids employees in navigating changes. This support ensures that the workforce remains resilient and adaptable, facilitating smoother transitions and sustained progress toward becoming a sentient enterprise.

Conclusion

Aligning organizational culture and structure with the principles of Sentient Marketing and AI-driven decision-making is pivotal for transforming into a sentient enterprise. Belief in innovation enables an organization to build a data-driven ecosystem, structure itself for agility, promote continuous learning, and manage change effectively.

By embracing these principles, businesses create an environment that supports and amplifies sentient enterprise practices. This approach enhances operational efficiency, improves customer experiences, and builds a sustainable competitive advantage for long-term success.

Chapter 10: The Future of Sentient Marketing

Imagine a world where marketing addresses your current needs and predicts your future desires. Products that fulfill your every whim instantly appear in your feed, and you only see offers that genuinely excite you. With the rapid progression of technology, the future of conscious marketing brims with thrilling potential.

This chapter explores the latest trends and technologies shaping the next stage of sentient marketing, providing insights on how businesses can lead the charge.

Predictive Technologies and AI

Predictive technologies and AI are poised to revolutionize how businesses understand and anticipate customer needs. By leveraging advanced predictive analytics, companies can forecast consumer behaviors and trends with greater accuracy. Enhanced algorithms will enable companies to predict what customers want before realizing it themselves. Integration with real-time data will allow businesses to respond to market changes instantly, ensuring they stay ahead of everyone else.

This capability transforms reactive marketing strategies into proactive ones, providing a significant competitive advantage.

Advanced Predictive Analytics

Enhanced algorithms will allow businesses to predict what customers want before they even realize it, achieving greater accuracy in forecasting consumer behaviors and trends. Integration with real-time data will enable businesses to respond to market changes instantly, staying ahead of the curve and meeting customer needs as they arise.

Predictive analytics will move beyond mere trend analysis, incorporating nuanced customer data to foresee subtle shifts in preferences and behavior. This granular level of prediction will support more personalized marketing efforts, driving higher engagement and conversion rates. The synergy between predictive analytics and real-time data will redefine the speed and precision of business responses to market dynamics.

AI-Powered Customer Insights

Advanced deep learning models will unlock profound insights into customer preferences and behaviors, giving businesses a competitive edge. Sophisticated behavioral analysis methods will clarify consumer motivations and actions, enabling more targeted and effective marketing.

By understanding the intricacies of customer journeys, businesses can tailor their interactions to match individual needs and preferences. AI-driven insights will also help identify emerging trends and untapped market segments, providing new growth opportunities. This deep understanding of customer behavior will foster stronger connections and more meaningful engagements, ultimately enhancing customer loyalty and satisfaction.

The Role of Automation in Marketing

Automation will streamline operations and enhance the precision of targeted campaigns. Future marketing automation platforms will feature intelligent campaign management, streamlining processes, and maximizing impact. Automation tools will ensure personalized content delivery, enhancing customer experience and engagement.

Businesses can focus on strategic activities that drive innovation and growth by automating routine tasks. Moreover, integrating AI in automation will enable more adaptive and responsive marketing strategies, ensuring that campaigns remain relevant in a constantly changing environment.

AI-Driven Chatbots and Virtual Assistants

Natural language processing (NLP) improvements will make chatbots and virtual assistants more conversational and context-aware, enhancing customer interactions. AI-driven tools will revolutionize customer support with instant, personalized assistance, elevating customer satisfaction and loyalty.

These virtual assistants will be capable of understanding complex queries and providing accurate, timely responses, improving the overall customer experience. Additionally, they will learn from each interaction, continuously improving their performance and personalization capabilities. This evolution in customer service will reduce wait times and increase the efficiency of support operations.

Hyper-Personalization

Hyper-personalization will take targeted marketing to a new level by focusing on individual customer needs and preferences. Advances in data analytics will allow for ultra-granular customer segmentation, enabling hyper-targeted marketing strategies that resonate deeply.

Individual-level personalization will surpass traditional segmentation, offering tailored experiences based on unique customer profiles. AI will generate personalized content at an unprecedented scale, from email copy to social media posts, ensuring each customer feels valued. Marketing efforts will dynamically adapt based on customer interactions and feedback, staying relevant and impactful.

Granular Customer Segmentation

Advances in data analytics will allow for ultra-granular customer segmentation, enabling hyper-targeted marketing strategies that resonate deeply. Individual-level personalization will surpass traditional segmentation, offering tailored experiences based on unique customer profiles. This deep level of segmentation will ensure that marketing messages are highly relevant and personalized, increasing engagement and conversion rates.

Businesses can precisely target niche audiences, maximizing their marketing campaigns' effectiveness. By creating accurate personas and segmenting based on behavior, companies can deliver more relevant and valuable experiences.

Dynamic Content Creation

AI will generate personalized content at an unprecedented scale, from email copy to social media posts, ensuring each customer feels valued. Marketing efforts will dynamically adapt based on customer interactions and feedback, staying relevant and impactful. This capability will allow businesses to maintain a consistent and personalized dialogue with their customers, enhancing engagement and loyalty. The ability to create and deliver dynamic content in real time will ensure that marketing messages are always fresh and relevant. Businesses can continuously optimize content based on customer behavior and achieve higher personalization and effectiveness.

Ethical AI and Responsible Marketing

Ethical AI and responsible marketing practices are essential to building and maintaining consumer trust. Ongoing efforts to mitigate bias in AI models will ensure ethical marketing practices that build trust and loyalty. Transparency and accountability in AI decision-making processes will foster a more profound customer connection.

As privacy concerns grow, businesses must implement robust measures to safeguard consumer information, building a foundation of trust. Ethical AI development will prioritize fairness and inclusivity, ensuring all customers are treated equitably. By adhering to moral principles, businesses can enhance their reputation and build stronger, more trusting relationships with their customers.

Ethical AI Development

Ongoing efforts to mitigate bias in AI models will ensure ethical marketing practices that build trust and loyalty. Transparency and accountability in AI decision-making processes will foster a more profound customer connection. Ethical AI development will prioritize fairness and inclusivity, ensuring all customers are treated equitably.

By adhering to moral principles, businesses can enhance their reputation and build stronger, more trusting relationships with their customers. Maintaining a solid ethical framework will be crucial to sustaining consumer confidence and trust as AI continues to evolve.

Consumer Privacy and Data Protection

As privacy concerns grow, businesses must implement robust measures to safeguard consumer information, building a foundation of trust. Transparent data practices and stringent security measures will reassure customers that their information is safe. Adopting privacy-by-design principles will ensure that data protection is integrated into every aspect of business operations. Regular audits and updates to data protection policies will help maintain compliance with evolving regulations. Businesses can enhance customer trust and foster long-term loyalty by prioritizing consumer privacy.

The Impact of Emerging Technologies

Emerging technologies like IoT and blockchain will redefine product marketing tactics. IoT data will enable hyper-contextual marketing, providing relevant content based on real-time environmental factors and enhancing the consumer experience. Blockchain technology will revolutionize data security, improving transparency and security and fostering greater trust between businesses and consumers.

Decentralized marketing platforms could disrupt traditional models, offering new opportunities for innovation. The integration of these technologies will create more dynamic and secure marketing strategies, driving greater efficiency and effectiveness.

Internet of Things (IoT)

IoT data will enable hyper-contextual marketing, providing relevant content based on real-time environmental factors and enhancing the consumer experience. Businesses can gather detailed insights into customer behavior and preferences by leveraging IoT devices. This data can be used to deliver personalized and timely marketing messages, increasing engagement and conversion rates.

IoT-enabled marketing will allow businesses to create more interactive and immersive experiences, connecting with customers in new and innovative ways. As IoT technology advances, its impact on marketing will only grow, offering exciting opportunities for businesses to differentiate themselves.

Blockchain Technology

Blockchain will revolutionize data security, enhancing transparency and security and fostering greater trust between businesses and consumers. Decentralized marketing platforms could disrupt traditional models, offering new opportunities for innovation. By leveraging blockchain, companies can ensure the integrity and security of their data, building greater trust with customers. Blockchain technology will also enable more transparent and accountable marketing practices, giving consumers greater control over their data. As blockchain adoption grows, its impact on marketing will be profound, driving greater efficiency and trust in business operations.

Preparing for the Future

Staying ahead in Sentient Marketing requires continuous investment in technology and a readiness to adapt. Businesses must continuously innovate to remain competitive. Developing in-house expertise in AI, data analytics, and other vital areas will harness the full potential of sentient marketing.

Adopting agile marketing strategies will allow businesses to adapt quickly to market changes, ensuring sustained success. Maintaining a consumer-centric approach ensures that technological advancements enhance the customer experience, driving loyalty and engagement.

Investing in Technology

Businesses must continuously innovate to remain competitive. Developing in-house expertise in AI, data analytics, and other vital areas will harness the full potential of sentient marketing. Investing in advanced technologies and tools will enable businesses to stay at the forefront of industry developments. Innovation thrives when the culture is open and flexible, and employees can explore new ideas and approaches. Continuous investment in technology will ensure businesses remain agile and flexible in emerging markets.

Adapting to Change

Focusing on the customer guarantees that technological innovations improve their experience, fostering loyalty and involvement. Companies can consistently update their approaches by keeping in touch with customer desires and tendencies. Agile methods will facilitate iterative progress and constant enhancement, helping businesses stay competitive. Accepting change and nurturing a culture of flexibility will be essential for lasting success in the evolving realm of sentient marketing.

Conclusion

The future of Sentient Marketing is filled with exciting possibilities driven by advancements in AI, automation, and emerging technologies. By staying informed about these trends and investing in the necessary capabilities, businesses can harness the power of Sentient Marketing to achieve unparalleled efficiency, personalization, and customer engagement.

Becoming a fully sentient enterprise requires continuous learning, adaptation, and innovation. Embrace the future enthusiastically and creatively, and watch your business thrive in this dynamic landscape.

Epilogue: The Human Touch

It's easy to feel overwhelmed by the constant media stories about AI taking over. However, let's set the record straight: humans are, and always will be, in control. This chapter is a heartfelt reminder that AI and advanced marketing technologies are tools to amplify our capabilities, not replace them. The beauty of Sentient Marketing lies in the synergy between human creativity and technological prowess.

Embrace Technology Without Losing Humanity

Since the dawn of civilization, humans have used tools to overcome challenges and expand our horizons. From the first stone tools to the advent of the internet, our ability to innovate and adapt has always set us apart. AI, machine learning, and generative AI are the latest in a long line of tools that, when wielded correctly, can help us achieve incredible things. These tools are only as powerful as the humans who design, control and use them.

AI excels at analyzing extensive data sets and detecting patterns that humans might miss. However, the human touch adds creativity, empathy, and context to these insights. AI provides the data, but humans craft the story and connect with others on a personal level. By automating repetitive tasks and providing deep insights, AI allows marketers to do their best: create, strategize, and build relationships. This synergy allows for more meaningful and impactful marketing efforts.

The Power of Human Connection

Connecting people to products is foundational to marketing. It's about listening to their needs, addressing their concerns, and offering solutions that improve their lives. While AI can analyze behaviors and predict trends, human empathy interprets these insights and translates them into genuine connections. Sentient

Marketing enables highly customized interactions, but the human touch ensures these interactions are heartfelt and meaningful.

When marketers understand and empathize with their audience, they can create experiences that resonate more deeply.

Trust is fundamental to any relationship, and it's developed through transparency, honesty, and mutual respect. AI can enhance these principles by offering precise data and insights, but the people behind the technology genuinely build trust through ethical behavior and authentic interaction.

The Ethical Stewardship of Technology

As custodians of advanced technologies, we are responsible for using them ethically. This means ensuring that our AI systems promote fairness, transparency, and respect for privacy. Humans must actively work to identify and mitigate biases in AI systems to prevent unfair treatment of any group. Protecting consumer data and respecting their privacy is paramount. Ethical data practices build trust and show that we value our customers beyond their data points.

Celebrating Human Ingenuity

Integrating AI into marketing isn't about replacing human ingenuity but enhancing it. Humans are the inventors, dreamers, and storytellers. AI can analyze and automate, but it cannot dream or inspire. The future of marketing will always depend on human creativity to push boundaries and explore new possibilities. Our ability to innovate, adapt, and empathize makes us unique. Sentient Marketing harnesses the power of AI to elevate our natural abilities, not overshadow them. By embracing technology as a partner, not a rival, we can achieve new heights of innovation and connection.

Conclusion

As we venture further into Sentient Marketing, let's remember that we are the architects of this field. AI and advanced technologies are our tools designed to serve our goals and enhance our capabilities. Our humanity—creativity, empathy, and ethical stewardship—sets us apart. By embracing the human touch in marketing, we allow technology to amplify our strengths and help us connect with others more profoundly and meaningfully.

AI is not taking over; we are in control. Harnessing these tools for good, creating, innovating, and connecting makes Sentient Marketing powerful. This approach involves using machines to unlock new possibilities, not replacing humans. Let's celebrate our unique ability to adapt and innovate, ensuring that the future of marketing remains human at its heart.